GROWING WILD MUSHROOMS

A Complete Guide to Cultivating Edible and Hallucinogenic Mushrooms

Revised with Color Photographs

by **Bob Harris**

Illustrated by **Susan Neri**

Photographs by Bob Harris & Alan Rockerfeller

Ronin Publishing, Inc.
Berkeley, CA
www.roninpub.com

Alan Rockefeller

Psilocybe cubensis

GROWING WILD MUSHROOMS

A Complete Guide to Cultivating Edible and Hallucinogenic Mushrooms

Revised with Color Photographs

by Bob Harris

Illustrated by Susan Neri

Photographs by Bob Harris & Alan Rockerfeller

Ronin Publishing, Inc.
Berkeley, CA
www.roninpub.com

Growing Wild Mushrooms
Copyright: 1976, 1978, 2018 by Bob Harris
Pbook ISBN: 9781579510664
Ebook ISBN: 9781579512279

Published by
RONIN Publishing, Inc.
PO Box 3436
Oakland CA 94609
www.roninpub.com

Printed in the United States of America
Distributed to the trade by PGW/ Ingram

Library of Congress Number: 26-6613

Table of Contents

GROWING WILD
MUSHROOMS

Psilocybe allenii

An Introduction to the Mushroom

THIS IS A book about you, me, and mushrooms. Just what is a mushroom? This basic question is a good place to begin. A mushroom is a class of fungi. Where are fungi found, and how do they grow? Although some of you may know some of the answers to these questions, let's talk about fungi in general before discussing specifically the various varieties of fungal fruits.

Fungi are plants and are unique in their specialization. They belong to a segment of life we call the *decomposers*. They lack chlorophyll, and thus cannot use direct sunlight for their energy as most plants do. Instead, they possess special enzymes and chemicals that decompose the life around them containing stored energy, usually in the form of sugars and starches. All fungi require some other organized life for their food support. Generally, fungi will be found living on wood, leaf mulch, or on soil in which the presence of dung provides a source of these sugars and starches.

Fungi are classified according to the type of relationship they have with their environment. If the fungus lives directly on the living organism without benefitting the host, we call this a *parasitic* relationship. If the fungus is living on dead material such as a tree stump, we call this second type of relationship *saprophytic*. A third type of relationship, in between these two, is called *mycorrhizal-symbiotic*. In this relationship the fungus is associated with the root of a green plant, but will not overcome it. In return for the supplying of certain chemicals or nutrients by the tree or plant the fungus breaks down other nutrients or interacts with metals making them utilizable by the tree or plant. Many of the fungi that have been discovered in recent years have been found to be mycorrhizal in their relationship. Understanding these basic life styles of fungi allows us to predict where we might best find mushrooms growing in the wild. Each species of mushroom inhabits a specific environment and is precise in the way that its chemistry is adapted to a specific host or environment. For example, the well known *Amanita muscaria* grows in association with the roots of pine or birch trees because it is mycorrhizal. In the case of the cultivated *Agaricus brunnescens*, a dung associated mushroom of the saprophytic type, we would look in a well manured pasture (see plate 2). The "honey mushroom", *Armillaria*, is a parasite which we would expect to find growing on a tree stump.

Let's talk more about the classification of fungi in order to understand the life cycle of the organism. Mushrooms are the most advanced form of fungi. When a botanist classifies a fungus as advanced or primitive, he is referring to its reproductive structures. Lower fungi, those that are considered more primitive, are generally simple in their organization. A spore germinates and cells grow out from the spore. The spores are organized into filaments we call *hyphae*. Each hypha has the capacity to divide and produce other hyphae. If one chops a hypha into pieces, each piece has the capacity to begin a new cycle and produce more hyphae. This principle of *vegetative reproduction* is basic to plants and distinguishes them from higher animals. When a group of hyphae grow and become a dense mat, whether on your Petri plate or in the wild, this is called *mycelium*. As the mycelium grows and develops, it produces stalks that bear spore-containing capsules called *sporangia*. These sporangia break open and release their spores, and the life cycle is complete. Examples of these lower forms of fungi are water molds, slimes, and things that rot out lawns and trees.

Climbing the complexity scale, we reach the higher fungi. These are divided into two groups, (1) the *Ascomycetes* and (2) the *Basidiomycetes*. The true mushroom is a Basidiomycete as are rusts, smuts and jelly fungi. The Ascomycetes, probably the largest and most well known class of fungi, includes yeasts, bread molds, penicillins, and a variety of different kinds of mushrooms, including the prized morel. The Ascomycetes are characterized by a spore-bearing sac called an *ascus*. Inside the ascus are 8 or fewer elongate spores called *ascospores*. The ascii are in turn found on the surface of a fruiting structure called an *ascocarp* and at the appropriate time the sacs break open and release all their spores. In the Basidiomycetes the spores form in a structure shaped like a cows udder called a *basidium* and the fruiting body is known as a *basidiocarp*, i.e., a mushroom (see fig. 1).

In these higher fungi, as with most of the plant kingdom, there is a vegetative and a reproductive part of the life cycle. In vegetative growth the spore germinates and grows out to form hyphae which in turn form mycelia. At this point you may find vegetative spores being formed. The hyphae will form a mat and a piece of reproductive tissue that has not undergone genetic reproduction. These spores can be germinated into hyphae to complete the vegetative cycle. When conditions are right, the second type of reproductive cycle

FIGURE 1

Ascomycete

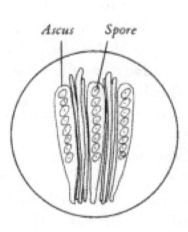

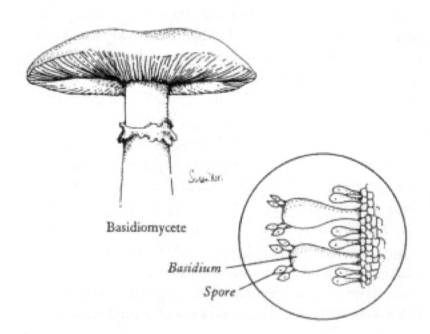

Basidiomycete

will occur. The hyphae continue on to form organized tissue, ascii or basidia, in which *meiosis* (genetic recombination) and chromosome reduction takes place. In each cell the number of chromosomes double and then separate leaving each new spore with a recombination of the genetic information.

Panaeolus cyanescens

Identification of plants is very often based on the reproductive structures, such as the flowers and fruit, the pollen, or the spores. When collecting mushrooms in the woods, we see only the reproductive structures and by studying these structures we are able to identify the various species. Since the mycelium is contained in the tree or underground, it is usually not visible. Generally, the mycelium will stay in the area and continue to grow as long as there are sufficient nutrients and proper conditions. During the weeks or months that the mycelium is hidden from view, it is digesting and spreading through the substrate, storing nutrients to be used in the burst of energy which sends forth the fruiting body.

When specific conditions are right it will send up the mushroom that we see. This spore-containing structure is called a *carpophore* (or an ascocarp; basidiocarp) and can be collected or observed through its spore deposit. The variation in the fruiting bodies is incredible and you will find fungi to be among the most beautiful creatures on the forest floor. Their growth rate is very rapid, especially in the case of the fungi that live in fields on manure or hay.

The chief factor in the growth and development of the fungi is water. In final form they are approximately 90% water. They need a high rate of humidity in order to germinate their spores and grow. This does not mean that the air has to be humid, although this helps. If you look at the forest floor many days after it has rained, you will find that under the top layer of leaves it is still very humid. In this layer of mulch there is a fairly constant amount of moisture in which bacteria and fungi grow. It is in this environment that we are most likely to find the fungi. With the necessary amount of water, the fungus can then activate all its chemicals and begin the process of decomposing animal or vegetable material that is already organized.

The role of the fungi is to prepare the material which has been organized in green plants or in animals for return to the earth, breaking down the nutrients which newly forming plants and animals can utilize. Fungi are a necessary part of nature, responsible for completion of the system and making it possible for some plants to live over thousands of years. The fungi don't do this alone but in conjunction with bacteria. When growing the commercial *Agaricus*, the common store mushroom, I found that it has an innate association with bacteria and other lower fungi. When one prepares the compost on which it is grown, there is a whole succession of lower organisms, both bacterial and fungal, which break down the cellulose before the straw and manure is acceptable to the mushroom. Once the compost is inoculated the mycelium requires the presence of certain algae and bacteria to form and stimulate the growth of the fruiting body. Thus throughout the entire life cycle, a fungus has an innate association with other decomposing organisms.

As a protection against some of these organisms, fungi often produce strong chemical compounds. These may be *bacteriostatic*, inhibiting the growth of certain bacteria in order to regulate the environment of the fungi. This is the source of such antibiotic chemicals as penicillin. Production of these chemicals is specific to the needs of the fungi for a specific environment, and various chemicals will be either present or absent accordingly. Plants, unlike animals, are unable to change their environment. Therefore they have developed a wide variety of chemicals in order to protect themselves and to allow for the continued survival and reproduction of their species. Man has found a great many uses for some of these chemicals. For instance, the yeasts that, under certain conditions, produce alcohol are the basis for a very large industry. Yeasts also produce vitamin B and are thus valuable nutritionally.

On the other hand, some of these chemicals which are produced by the fungi have no known reason for their existence. Some of the poisons found in the *Amanita* varities have no known relationship to the protection of the organism or regulation of its environment. Yet they are very complex and potent poisons. Obviously, many of these fungi are not for human consumption.

It is absolutely critical that each person who decides to become involved with fungi takes the time to educate himself thoroughly. This is not restricted to classes taken at a university, for there are most definitely other sources of information. Your local Mycological Society would be a good place to start. When going into the woods to identify fungi, it is necessary to have a person along who has training or background in fungi identification and a thorough familiarity with a field guide. It takes time to learn to identify various fungi, each with its own set of characteristics. It was once my good fortune to go on a mushroom hunt with a band of professional mycologists led by the famous mushroom authority, Dan Stuntz. Such a hunt is called a *foray*, and its purpose is to collect and discuss as many species as possible in order to broaden the understanding of all. I was most impressed with this expert's ability to greet each mushroom anew and either identify it or, refraining from absolute identification, give out what knowledge he had. When wandering through the splendor of the woods, you must gain or regain this kind of childlike curiosity. With an open and sensitive search and a keen, receptive mind, you will soon be able to get a feeling for the relations between various species of fungi and their environments. Once you have an understanding of this relationship, you can then make periodic trips into the woods during the rainy season and see fungi fruiting again and again. Many of them will continue to come up in the same spot in which you have previously found them, making less work for the hunter. In the case of the fairy ring mushroom, we know that they continually grow out of an area where a tree has been. Year after year, the nutrients are digested by the fairy ring and the circle grows larger and larger. In the case of the fungi that grow

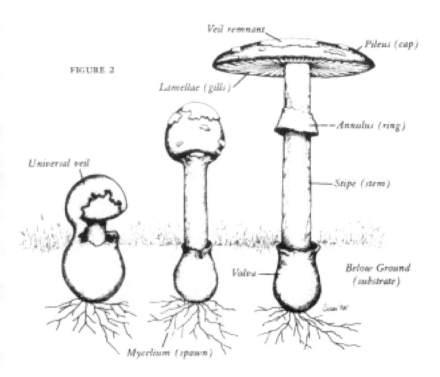

FIGURE 2

Veil remnant

Pileus (cap)

Lamellae (gills)

Annulus (ring)

Universal veil

Stipe (stem)

Volva

Below Ground (substrate)

Mycelium (spawn)

directly on wood, such as oyster mushrooms, or "chicken-of-the-woods", we need only come back each year to see it growing out of the same tree. Generally, the mycologist will go into the woods looking for certain fungi at certain times of the year knowing which will be evident. By having some such authority along, you will know which mushroom is best left in the ground, and which to take home to the dinner table.

In order to identify the fungus, we will have to identify which structures are distinguishing factors. Involved in this identification process are the names of the various structures and parts of the mushroom (see fig 2). A true mushroom, as we know it, is a Basidiomycete. This means that the spores arise on udder-like structures on the gills under the cap of the mushroom (see fig. 1). The stalk of the mushroom is called a *stipe*. The gills of a mushroom are called *lamellae* and contain *hymenia*, which is the fruiting and support structure for the basidia which bear the spores. The cap is called the *pileus*. When the mushroom is small, there may be a *veil*, a sheath covering the gills. When the mushroom gets older and this veil breaks, it may stay on the stipe or form a ring around it called an *annulus*. There is a wide variation among species however, and many do not have what is called a persistent veil or annulus. Many mushrooms do not even have true gills. For the most part we will be talking about mushrooms that do have gills, and the botanical family in which they are located is called *Agaricaceae*. Some of the *Agaricaceae* at the small button stage are encapsulated in a sheath called a *volva*. This is true of all the *Amanita* genus. As the mushroom grows larger, the volva breaks and there remains usually an annulus or a veil and a cup deep in the soil at the base of the stipe. It is important to learn the names of the structures, but not necessarily the scientific names. "Gills" is as good as lamellae; "stem" as good as stipe; "ring" as good as annulus.

I have been collecting for five years and am only a beginner at identifying the wild fungi. I am gradually learning to see the wide variation that exists in these basic structures. In some cases, the particular structure may not be present. In other cases the same structure may be exaggerated or amply present. Look carefully at each specimen and examine each structural part.

A very helpful method of identifying fungi is to make a spore print. To do this, set the mushroom cap on a piece of paper and cover it with a bowl overnight. Upon lifting the

Alan Rockefeller

Figure 3 Spore Print

cap, you will see that the spores have been discharged on to the paper leaving the distinguishing spore print (see fig. 3). Each family has a different color and arrangement of spores. In gilled fungi, the spores are found on the surface of the gills.

An additional way of identifying different families is by breaking the cap in half and noting the pattern in which the gills are formed. You will find that certain gill patterns are characteristic to certain families. The gills, which run from the edge of the cap towards the stem, may stretch all the way from the stem to the edge; only half way; or even less. In some species, all of the gills will be of the same kind. In other species, there will be a mixture in the kinds of gills. The shape of the gill as it is attached to the stem is also important. This is known at the *gill pattern* (see fig. 4). The first type of attachment of the gill to the stipe is called *free* (fig. 4-A). In the free type the gill stretches from the *margin*, or the edge of the cap, to the very top of the stem. However, it does not attach directly to the stem, but rather to the point at which the stem meets the cap. The second type of gill pattern is called *adnate* (fig. 4-B) or squarely attached. Here gills run directly from the margin horizontally to the stem and attach directly to the stem. In the *adnexed* type (fig. 4-C), the gills run from the margin to the stem and then take a slight jog upward into the top of the stem. Another type is

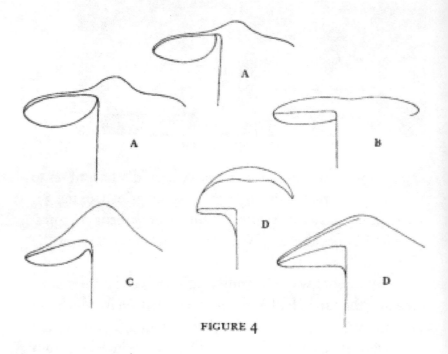

FIGURE 4

called *decurrent* (fig. 4-D). The gills in this case come from the margin and bend down along the stem and then attach to the stem.

There are other terms to describe the shape of this attachment. There is the *sinuate* shape, in which there is a slight depression upward in the gill before it attaches to the stem. These terms describe the shape of the gill if one breaks or cuts the stem and looks at the gills from the side. In looking at the radial arrangement, one will find that there will be some partial gills in some cases. The gills will be thicker or thinner depending on the species and there will be either wider or narrower separations. These different characteristics play a key role in identifying the mushroom.

In addition, the shape of the cap as a whole is very important. There will be wide variation within a species, but it will only be within certain limitations. Some fungi will be

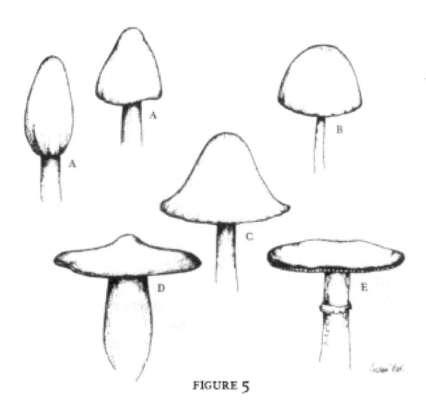

FIGURE 5

shaped more or less like cones (fig. 5-A). Others will be hemispherically shaped (fig. 5-B). Some will be convex or a little less hemispherical, more flattened out, and some will be bell-shaped (fig. 5-C). Some will have tips on the top, nipple-like protrusions called *umbos*, or umbonate (fig. 5-D). Some will be flat on the top (fig. 5-E). Some will be raised at the edge, and some will curl in at the edge, or margin. Within these parameters, you can begin to identify species from the shape of their caps. Further identification can then be made from the gill patterns and finally from the spore print. The size of the cap and the length and width of the stem are characteristic to a particular fungus. I have found chantrelles to range from the size of my thumb to a weight of five pounds. I have found puff balls as small as my fist and as big as basketballs. After some experience in collecting a particular species, you will get a feeling for the capacity and limitations of that species.

When collecting, you should try to get a clear picture of the stages that a mushroom goes through from youth to maturity. If you find a good collection spot with a good sample, you will generally see a mature, a young, and an intermediate stage. Often the young fungi will look nothing like the larger, more mature version. You might see a change in color, a change in size and a change in the shape of the cap. For example, there are field mushrooms that are covered with a slimy film called a *viscid pellicle* (see photo pg. 78). With many fungi, you can take the cap between your fingers, squeeze a piece of the edge, and then proceed to tear off the thin mucilaginous film from the cap. This is the pellicle. If you go out on a rainy day and find field mushrooms of this variety, you can readily see this. If you come back to the same spot after the sun has been shining for two days, you will see that what was a brown sticky mushroom has turned into a white smooth mushroom with an almost dried feeling to the skin (see plate 4). Noting characteristics by breaking the stem is also a manner of identification. In some cases the stems are hollow and in others, solid. Some stems will break easily and some will bend and seem elastic. The color of the juice that comes out of the broken stem is to be noted. In some cases there will be milk formed, as in the case of the *Lactarius* genus.

Texture is a very important quality to be used in identification. The mushroom may be slimy and viscid like the cap of the Slippery Jack Boletus, or have a tufted hairy quality as does the Shaggy Mane, *Coprinus comatus* (see plate 1).

Hericium erinaceus

Alan Rockerfeller

Certain fungi when bruised will turn different colors. Some
will turn yellow, some blue, and some will turn red. These
are frequently used indicators provided that all of the other
characteristics are the same. Often the trained botanist will
note odors that are particular to certain families. Some fungi
smell awful. Therefore we can use all of our senses: our sight
to identify structural parts, our sense of touch used to feel the
texture, our sense of smell and our sense of taste, although
tasting should be reserved until identification determines
the mushroom not to be of a poisonous variety. There are
even fungi that make noises. When picked some of the big
red and yellow cup fungi if put to the ear will make a hissing
sound which is a product of their spores being released. For
the purpose of identification, the sense of hearing is the least
useful, while touch, sight and smell are of great assistance.

Although the scientist may be less inclined to use the senses as a means of identification, they have been used for thousands of years and actually are quite sufficient.

While I have been collecting for several years, there are often many fungi in the woods that I do not know because I have not learned either the macro or micro characteristics. I learn one species of fungus at a time. I spend a day or several days collecting that one until I really know it. A species that I collected in Oregon took me a full day to identify the characteristics. I had been given several different descriptions and I found that there was great variation in the shape of the cap. In some cases it resembled the species that I was hunting and in others a poisonous variety. It was only after a long search that I determined the chief characteristic to be the pellicle.

A Note on Cultivation

I HAVE DISCUSSED briefly what mushrooms are and something about their habitat and characteristics. Before I begin a detailed description of how to cultivate them, I would like to describe the general requirements for such work. Since mushrooms derive their food from composting substances it is necessary to provide them with food. Since the foods used for growing mushrooms are so rich and full of nutrients one must make sure that only the desired fungus will be growing on this food or medium. To do this requires killing all the bacteria and fungal life normally present in the food. This process is called *sterilization* and is the essence of mushroom culture. Simply, a sealed container with nutrients in it is subjected to high temperature for a period of time, which kills all life. Then a piece of the mushroom mycelium is introduced into the medium without allowing any foreign spores from other fungi into the container. Such techniques are called *sterile transfers* and require the conditions and procedures that will be outlined step by step in the proceeding chapters. The mycelium for this culturing can come from existing cultures, spores, or directly from the cap of a fresh mushroom. Before one can start these cultures, however, it is necessary to have an area set aside for sterile transfers of mycelium, a means of sterilization and the proper nutrients on which to start the culture. Let us begin to discuss in detail the exact conditions for this work.

Equipment for Sterile Culture Work

STERILE CULTURE work requires a special area set aside solely for sterile work. This area should be (1) draft-free, and (2) germ-free. The degree of success in producing a pure, contamination-free culture will depend on the ability to ensure these conditions while opening a sterile container. Since the sterile containers are usually filled with very rich food sources or substrates, any spores which do enter while the container is open are likely to produce a second undesirable culture. These secondary organisms frequently compete more successfully for the food than the one which is desired. Therefore it is important to have a work area in which there are fewer chances for these "weeds" or contaminants to get inside the containers during inoculation.

The least sophisticated way to do this is in a small room with the windows and doors shut. You can then take a small piece of glass or a smooth table top (formica, etc.) and wash it down with Lysol or Hexol, or any disinfectant, and then wipe it with alcohol. When inoculating, wear a gauze face mask, and work quickly, but gently. With this method, you can insure a fair success with cultures. One simply compromises in using an unsophisticated transfer area with throwing out a few contaminated cultures.

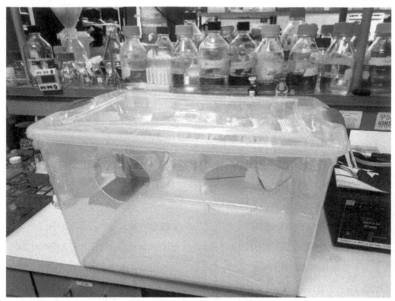

Alan Rockerfeller

Glove Box

TRANSFER CHAMBER OR GLOVE BOX

However, for more serious work, you should construct a chamber. This is simply an enclosed surface that can be cleaned with disinfectants to keep out contaminants. For myself, I add a germicidal UV (ultraviolet) fluorescent lamp, but I think you can achieve good results without this. The UV lamp only works on bacteria, not fungi. (The DNA structure in bacteria is sensitive to UV light and is destroyed by it, while fungi are not.) Such a chamber can be designed in many ways. Mine looks a bit like figure 6.

There is a strip of plywood across the front below the plexiglass. There is an opening below the plywood strip which is covered by a piece of hanging fabric. In this way, you can put your hands inside the chamber, and the cloth will drape down over your arms while you are working in the box — effectively keeping out drafts. When using the cloth-covered type chamber it is best to wash one's hands with alcohol before working. Other people prefer to make a true glove box. That is a chamber completely closed except for a door on the side and two holes in front onto which two rubber gloves have been permanently attached inside the box. I find this unnecessarily cumbersome, but it does work extremely well.

The tools required to do transfer work are simple — an alcohol lamp or bunsen burner, a wire loop and a knife. (See fig. 11) The wire loop can be a piece of nichrome wire (the wire used in toasters and electric heaters) which is carried by many electric appliance repair stores. Twist this into a loop and put it in a pin-vise or into one of those lead pencils used in mechanical drawing that clamp on to the piece of lead. The knife can be a small Exacto knife or a piece of broken razor blade stuck into a pin-vise.

STERILIZER

To free the media (the food for the fungus) of unwanted spores, it is necessary to sterilize them. An autoclave is a device used to heat things up under pressure in order to sterilize them. All pressure cookers do this. By heating water under pressure, the temperature of water can be made to go higher than 212°F, in fact as high as 250°F or more. By heating media up to 250°F for 20 to 40 minutes, one can effectively kill all spores and organisms. The most effective type of pressure cooker for my use has turned out to be a

21-quart model made of aluminum with a lid held by screw handles and with a pressure gauge on top. The cost is around forty-five dollars and it works wonderfully. In order to get an accurate pressure reading, be careful, before sealing the lid, to let the temperature go up and down slowly so that the steam can flow out.

Now, with a pressure cooker and a transfer chamber, you can begin work by preparing the nutrients in sterile form.

Media

In growing fungi, there are often various media on which a single culture will grow. The choice of media depends upon the desired use of the medium. Classically, three different types of media are used at various stages in the process of isolation, spawn production, and cultivation. These are agar media, grain media, and compost. Each has its advantages and disadvantages and therefore proper usage.

MAKING AND POURING AGAR MEDIA

The first is agar media. These are used to isolate single cultures and also frequently for long term storage of cultures. Agar is a sea weed extract that when made with hot water in 1.5-2%, or higher percent solution(s), will form a jellied texture upon cooling. Different nutrients are added to this solution according to the specific fungus and its needs. Some media will be specific for only a few fungi; others will be able to grow many varied kinds. By adding selective nutrients one can make the right mixture for the right organism.

In growing different mushrooms I have tried various media and many are a bit better, but not by far, than potato dextrose yeast, i.e., potato soluble starch, nutritional yeast and corn sugar with 1.5% (by weight) agar. Almost every wild mushroom will grow on this. No other ingredients are really necessary.*

AGAR MEDIA FOR PETRI PLATES AND SLANTS:

For Basidiomycetes:

2% Malt

H_2O	1 l	500 ml
Malt Powder	20 gms	10 gms
Corn Steepwater	20 ml	10 ml
$Ca(OH)_2$	.2 gm	.1 gm
(Calcium hydroxide)		
K_2HPO_4	.3 gm	.1 gm
(Potassium phosphate, dibasic)		
Agar Agar	20 gms	10 gms

Care must be used with malt media not to exceed 10 pounds pressure for 20 minutes. Higher temperatures cause the malt sugars to caramelize, preventing the agar from jelling properly.

PDY (Potato Dextrose Yeast)

Potato Water	1 l	500 ml
Dextrose	20 gms	10 gms
(Corn Sugar)		
Nutritional Yeast	6 gms	3 gms
Agar Agar	15 gms	7.5 gms

Potato water is prepared by boiling a large scrubbed, but not peeled, potato in water for one hour. It is cut into one inch slices prior to boiling and strained out leaving the potato water.

*It is, however, important to make sure the acidity or pH of the medium is correct. Most mushrooms prefer a neutral to slightly acid range. That is, a pH of about 5.5 to 6.5. The potato dextrose medium is in this range with no additions. The malt cornsteep water has some neutralizing agents in it to make and maintain the correct pH during the growth of the mycelium.

V-8 Oatmeal

Water	1 l	500 ml
V-8 Juice	50 ml	25 ml
Cream of Oats	50 gms	25 gms
Agar Agar	20 gms	10 gms

Here be careful to use a container much larger than the volume of medium. I.e., prepare a 500 ml medium in 2 liter flasks or it will tend to boil over no matter how slowly it is cooled down.

To use this agar medium for the isolation of fungi it should be poured in a thin layer on a wide dish. This is why Petri plates are classically used. They are 2½-5 inches across and ½ inch high at the most. This gives a wide, easily accessible surface. If a culture is started on this agar plate and contamination occurs, you can easily open the plate, remove the desired fungus by cutting out a small cube of agar with a sterile knife and transfer it to another plate or another medium. On the other hand, because of the large exposure of the Petri plate, it can easily be subject to contamination. This makes it only desirable for experimentation or for isolation.

The process of sterilizing and pouring agar deserves some comment. First, the nutrients are put into a container and sterilized. The best shape for doing this is an Erlenmeyer flask (see fig. 7).

This size flask should be able to hold about two times the quantity of medium used. In other words, a 500 ml batch of medium should be prepared in a one liter container. (A liter is about one quart.) The opening of the Erlenmeyer flask is sealed with a gauze-covered cotton plug. I then cover this with a piece of aluminum foil (recyclable). I put all the chemicals and powders (dry) in the flask, add the liquids,

Alan Rockerfeller

FIGURE 7

and pressure sterilize. It is suggested however, that the agar be allowed to sit at least thirty minutes in the liquid to condition it before sterilizing. Agar does not dissolve easily in even warm water — therefore, it is necessary to get the water almost to the boiling point before it will dissolve. Once it is in solution, it must be cooled off to almost 100°F before it gels or solidifies. This then affords ample time to pour the sterilized agar into pre-sterilized Petri plates or test tubes. The shape of the Erlenmeyer flask is very desirable as it has a small neck that can easily be held while pouring a controlled amount into each container. The agar medium is then sterilized at ten to twelve pounds of pressure for twenty minutes.

Now all is ready. Sterilized Petri plates are laid out flat in the disinfected transfer chamber. (Note: glass Petri plates are wrapped in aluminum foil, sterilized and allowed to cool; when ready to use, they are unwrapped and placed in the transfer chamber and should be used that day. Or use

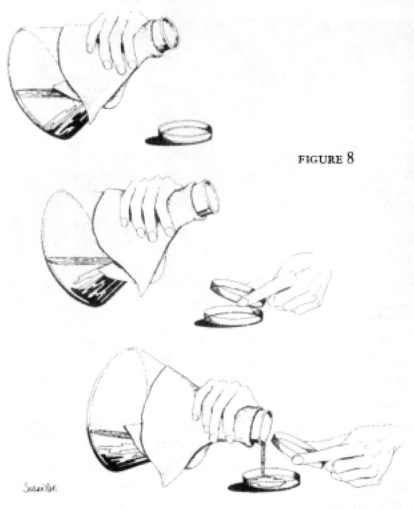

pre-sterilized plastic ones — five cents apiece.) The foil is removed and the Erlenmeyer flask is also put in the transfer chamber. Now with hands washed with alcohol, remove the cotton plug and tip the neck of the flask over to pour it. From now until it is put down again, the flask should always be held at a slight angle, i.e., not with the throat vertical. This decreases the chances of entry by contaminating spores. With the other hand, open the lid of the Petri plate, and hold it above the bottom plate at an angle. (See fig. 8)

Pour a thin layer in the bottom and quickly but gently place the cover plate over the bottom. With practice one can pour and move plates around without having to put the flask down. In the event that one must put it down, the cotton plug should be replaced in the flask — avoid touching the sterile inside part of the plug. I generally place the cotton plug on a thoroughly disinfected tile square. It is advantageous not to spill medium on the transfer chamber bottom; its richness is a haven for spores. In the event medium is spilled, a clean paper towel dampened with alcohol can be used to wipe it off. Then, return to pouring.

There is one other classical use of agar media, that being long term storage of cultures. This, however, is done by using containers with small orifices, such as a test tube. In using agar media in test tubes, the agar is allowed to cool and gel in such a way that it forms a long sloping surface called a "slant". (See fig. 9)

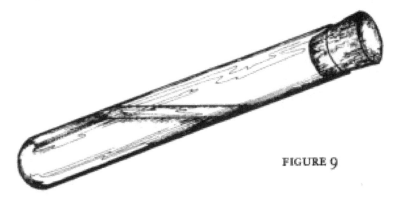

FIGURE 9

By doing this, you have a container with a small opening which is difficult to contaminate. It is, however, hard to maneuver in this narrow space, so it is inconvenient for experimentation or isolation.

Many higher fungi do not form sexual fruiting bodies (i.e., mushrooms) on agar, but readily form mycelial (vegetative) growth, which further suits agar media for isolation or storage, but not for the formation of fruiting bodies.

GRAIN MEDIA

Once a fungus (the desired mushroom) has been successfully isolated on an agar medium and a pure culture of it has been grown in duplicate on an agar slant and put away for security's sake, it is desirable to transfer a culture of it to grain medium. This is due to a rather peculiar nature observed in fungi. Fungi grown on agar will not move onto grain or compost until it has covered the agar cube. Transferring an agar culture directly onto compost results in a time lag and is, therefore, wasteful. Instead, the fungus is grown on grain from the agar. There is a time lag here too, although once it begins to grow out on the grain, the sterile containers of the grain can be shaken, facilitating the spread of the fungus through the grain. Once grown out on the grain, it can be readily transferred to the compost.

Rye or Milo Medium

3 gms $Ca(OH)_2$ per gallon H_2O
⅔ cup of H_2O (with $Ca(OH)_2$) for one cup grain

Sterilize 45 minutes at 15 pounds pressure.

The grain medium of choice is simply rye or milo (a sorghum grain similar to millet) plus some KOH (Potassium hydroxide, $Ca(OH)_2$ (Calcium hydroxide) or $CaCO_3$ (limestone) to correct for pH (acidity of the solution). The proper pH is 5.5-6.5 for most mushrooms. Other things such as vitamin B, or cornsteep liquor can be added but are not necessary. The grain and liquid are placed in a suitable container. I generally use clear soda pop bottles with cotton plugs. Commercial spawn producers use half gallon narrow mouth Mason jars with a cap having a 1½ inch hole and a special cloth-asbestos filter fitting into the cap. A few years ago glass milk bottles with plugs in them were used. I then sterilize the grain and water for forty-five minutes at fifteen pounds pressure. When the pressure is down, remove the bottles and shake them so that the grains are separated. Then set them aside to cool. When cooled they can be inoculated with fungus; however, they should be shaken just prior to opening for inoculation.

In-vitro Mushroom Jars

Vancouver Seed Bank

The grain-grown fungus in the jars or bottles should be shaken every four to five days to spread the mycelium and get it to completely encapsulate each individual grain.

I would like to add that I sometimes place a small amount of grain medium in test tubes. I then inoculate this with agar-grown fungi. The fungus grown on the grain in the test tube can be readily transferred to the next step (bottles or jars) with little fear of contamination. I have found, with wider-mouthed containers, that the mycelium can grow out, apparently free of foreign growths, to cover the substrate. Contaminating spores often get in later, however, and rest on the surface of the medium which is completely engulfed by the fungus. When this mycelium is transferred to a new medium, the contaminating spores germinate and lead to endless hassles. It is interesting that when the mycelium completely covers the substrate, it is quite resistant to contamination problems. Though the foreign spores may be present, they rarely germinate under such conditions.

COMPOST

Once enough inoculum is grown out on grain medium, it can be used to inoculate a properly composted straw and manure heap (or some similar vegetable/nitrogen-high mixture — e.g., tobacco stalks, etc.) Actually, you can *case** a jar in which the fungus has engulfed the grain and force it to fruit, which is to send up a mushroom from mycelium, in culture. A sterilized mixture of sand, $CaCO_3$, vermiculite and peat moss is one type of casing material. A ½-1 inch thick layer over the grain, kept moist, will, in some cases,

*Casing the mycelium is a mushroom-growing technique in which the mycelium is covered with a layer of non-nutritive soil.

induce copious fruiting. Since cultivation of the mycelium on sterile grain is so labor intensive, for most practical purposes it is advantageous to use compost for the actual fruiting of the mushrooms.

Alan Rockefeller

Laetiporus sulphureus

In California when Laetiporus sulphureous grows on Eycalyptus–which is where you'll usually see it–it is toxic and can cause stomach upset.

There are some very sophisticated ways and techniques of composting aerobically in order to get the proper substrate for mushrooms. All life is a succession of organisms. Essentially, composting establishes ideal conditions for bacteria and fungi to convert some of the starches and cellulose into sugars and amino acids, etc., which are then usable by fungi. In a compost heap, bacterial work is followed by a rise in temperature. Thermophilic bacteria and fungi, which can only live at high temperatures (e.g., 80-125°F), begin to multiply at this point. They, in turn, are succeeded by other organisms able to work at still higher temperature ranges, 120-140° and 140-175°F. By this succession, straw is broken down, nitrogen assimilated and sugars made available on which Basidiomycetes can survive. The process of turning a compost heap is performed to get a uniform mixture throughout the heap of the proper air and moisture for these organisms to work.

It is essential to start with materials of the right chemical composition and structural size or shape. Straw and manure will do, for many mushrooms. Partially shredded or chopped straw will absorb moisture and provide texture for aeration. The manure provides nitrogen. Most often all the spores to perform the composting are right in the hay or manure, so you needn't add any commercial inoculators. The hay must be thoroughly soaked in the week or so before starting and the manure should be fresh and free of ammonia. The compost is then stacked in a heap, layering manure and straw. The size of the heap is a function of where you live. In New England in winter a heap should be 8' high with an 8'×8' base. San Francisco needs only a 6' high heap. The height is chosen to insure the insulation of the center of the pile to keep the heat inside. Once stacked, a heap is covered with plastic — mostly to keep rain from leaching out soluble nutrients, as it does little to keep heat in or prevent evaporation except off the top layers. Actually if the rainfall does not last too many days the outer layer of straw will repel the water very successfully.

Generally if all is proceeding well the heap will rise to 130-160°F within five to seven days.* It is then turned by moving

*The temperature of a heap can be measured by inserting a simple candy thermometer one foot down into the top of the heap.

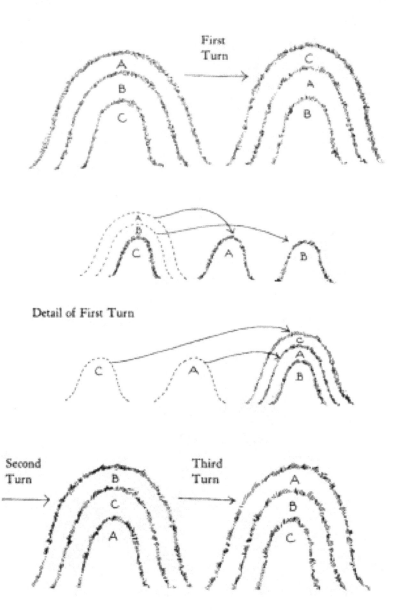

First
Turn

Detail of First Turn

Second
Turn

Third
Turn

FIGURE 10

the middle ⅓ to the bottom, the bottom to the new top and the top to the new middle. (See fig. 10) It is allowed to heat up again for about one week and then turned again using the same technique. One more turn a week later should complete the mixing but if the temperature is still above 130° turn it a fourth time. Each turning usually requires a watering — a super fine misting nozzle is perfect to moisten, not soak, the heap. When done the heap should be brown to gold, the hay easily splitable and sweet smelling, and a handful should compact easily without being runny. If it is properly prepared, the compost can then be filled in boxes and tamped down or spread on the ground. It is then sprinkled with grain-grown spawn and covered with a thin layer of compost. A sheet of plastic should be placed over it and it should be allowed to sit for four to five weeks, perhaps gently sprinkling once weekly. It is then cased and watered gently daily keeping the soil moist but not wet until mushrooms appear.

Shoomery

Straw and Manure Substrate

In the compost piles that we have been running, we used a mixture of straw and dairy manure. In this particular case we were using a ratio of about ten bales of straw weighing about forty pounds each to one-half pick-up load of fresh manure. The straw, I'd like to emphasize, was shredded. You must shred half of the straw, in this case approximately five bales. You may build, buy or borrow a shredder or use a rotary lawn mower to run over the straw. And you must have the proper amount of water. The shredding and watering are critical factors. The straw we used was dried, so we spread it over the open ground about ten inches thick and watered it once or twice a day covering it with plastic in between. If it were thicker than ten inches, the water would not penetrate the straw. In a dry climate or season it is very difficult to get enough water into the straw to obtain the necessary humidity because it is covered with a waxy surface. By watering it frequently, once or twice a day, and covering it with any type of plastic, it will tend to soak up enough

Shredded straw

water. We did this for about a week and got a really wet condition. When you are turning piles by hand it is necessary to take the time to get the necessary amount of water into it in the initial stage before you add the manure (the nitrogen).

Dairy Manure Mushroom Substrate

Dairy manure is an adequate manure for many, but not all, mushrooms. The manure that we were using in these experiments came fresh from a dairy farm. They had taken it directly out of a barn with a pump system. We then strained the water off, leaving the manure quite moist and easy to spread in between the layers of straw. I suggest that if you have manure that is somewhat dried out that you mix this manure with water. A kind of cement can be made out of it so that you can spread a rather wet layer of manure across the straw as you are layering it.

On the day that you have decided that your straw is wet enough, (it should just about — but not quite — squeeze water out in your hands), get fresh manure and stack it, alternating a thin layer of manure with a thick (8-12 inches) layer of straw. Continue to build your stack that way. The more rectangular, or straighter, the sides of the stack are, the better. It is difficult to build a straight stack by hand, so you are likely to wind up with a mound shape, as in fig. 10.

The initial turnings of the pile will require more water than the later turnings. In this first turning with the cow manure it is really a good idea to get as much water into it as possible. Water and oxygen are the rate limiting factors for the bacteria and the fungi in the compost heap. This means that deprived of either enough moisture or enough oxygen the compost will not favor the thermophilic, cellulitic organisms that are necessary to produce the right compounds for the Basidiomycetes, the mushrooms, to grow in.

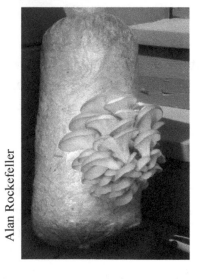

Alan Rockefeller

Pleurotus ostreatus

There are some mushrooms which live on other substrates not requiring composting. For example, the oyster mushroom, *Pleurotis ostreatus*, can live on composted straw or on magazine scraps or wood chips. Or the spawn grown on grain can be placed in holes drilled in oak logs. Experimentation with different manures and vegetable matter will quickly yield the cultivation requirements of a fungus provided you have enough spawn available.

INDOOR AND SMALL QUANTITY COMPOST PRODUCTION.

In the previous section, I have described the methods for making a compost pile. Often this is not possible. However, if you have a shed, garage or basement, smaller amounts of compost can be made. Using the same ratios and principles described previously, compost can be made in a small compost bin, such as the Rotocrop (see photo). Because of the shape and design, as little as one bale of straw can be composted.

In the event that one desires a smaller amount of compost done in a precise fashion, James P. San Antonio of the Department of Agriculture has perfected a method using a styrofoam picnic basket, with a variable transformer to control the steam and compost temperature. The final product is about 3 gallons of pure pasteurized compost in just 6–7 days.

The construction of the compost maker utilizes a styrofoam picnic basket, preferably 14 inches by 22 inches by 15 inches deep. Six ¾ inch holes, evenly spaced across the surface, are cut into the lid with a knife. Six more holes of the same size are cut in the basket (three on each of the long sides) two inches up from the bottom. On the short sides of the basket, one hole is cut on each side at the bottom edge. One hole is ½ inch and will serve for drainage. The other end has a hole ¾ inch wide and 2½–3 inches deep to ac-

commodate the head of the vaporizer unit. Line the bottom
with aluminum foil.

Next, a screen support is made from ¼ inch screen so that
it sits 4 inches up from the bottom of the chest. Make sure
there is clearance in the screen for the vaporizer head. The
compost sits on this screen so that the steam can flow evenly
under the compost.

Finally, a hose is clamped to a one-gallon jug which is
placed upside down in a ring stand. A 1½ inch hole is cut

in the reservoir of the vaporizer to accommodate the hose. The vaporizer is filled to the "fill" line and the hose inserted so that the open end of the hose rests ½ inch below the fill line. In this way, a constant level of water is maintained in the reservoir, which makes the steam output constant. I should add here that the vaporizing electrodes *must* be cleaned at least every other day (according to the manufacturer's directions) or the output of steam will be grossly affected.

Before beginning a compost run, it is best to hook up the vaporizer to the variable transformer (set on full voltage). Put adhesive tape over all the holes except for the one for the vaporizer head and allow the basket to steam for 4–6 hours to eliminate the plastic odors.

To begin the compost run, mix approximately 3 gallons of shredded dry stable manure (with straw) in a bucket or plastic bag with 3–4 ounces of cottonseed meal, or 1–2 ounces of blood meal. Add 3½ quarts of hot water (about 70°C) to this mixture, preferably with a sprayer to assure thorough mixing. This warm mixture is put in the picnic basket without delay, loosely filling the basket to within 1–2 inches of the top. Five sticks are placed in the basket before adding

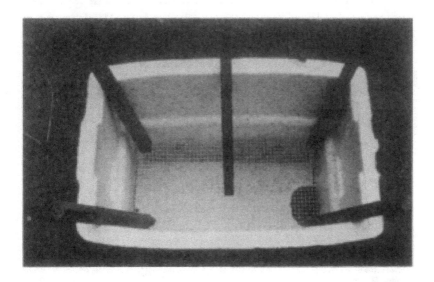

the compost so that after the compost is added a two inch ventilation shaft can be created by moving the stick around. The sticks are removed, the lid placed on the top, the transformer set on full voltage, and all the holes taped shut except for one of the holes in the lid farthest from the vaporizer head. A thermometer is placed in this hole so that it is in the middle of the compost.

During this phase pasteurization occurs, killing all the insect life. Note that this is opposite to how it is done at a

mushroom farm where pasteurizing takes place at the end
of the composting. After about two hours, the temperature
should rise to 70°C. Note that the settings described for the
transformer are different under different circumstances, so
use this data only as a guide. What is important is to get
your unit to reach the temperatures described. Once the temperature rises above 60°C, check the time and let the compost stay above 60°C for 3–4 hours.

At the end of this time, remove all the pieces of tape from
the holes to allow the compost to ventilate. Within a day,
ammonia will be noticeable in the exhaust steam and the
temperature should be 55–65°C. Hold this temperature for
two or three full days. After the first day, the ammonia odor
should disappear. After this happens, white fire fang, or
actinomycete fungi, are apparent in the compost. At the end
of this time, these fungi should be prominent. The voltage is
then lowered a few volts at a time so that the temperature
drops in the compost to 45–55°C—a few degrees every 2–3
hours is a sufficient drop rate. The compost is then held 3–4

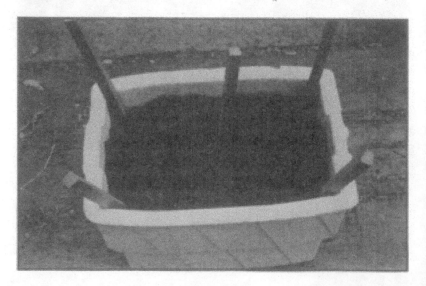

days at this lower temperature. At the end of this time, the transformer is turned off and the compost allowed to cool in the basket slowly, say over 6 hours. The compost is ready for inoculation when it cools to 24–28°C.

The compost made in this fashion is usually excellent and has the added benefit that the mixture can be easily controlled. One extra is that the drain water from the small hole makes excellent organic fertilizer for your plants.

Mushroom Photo Plates

Bob Harris

PLATE 1   Wild *Coprinus comatus*

Bob Harris

Alan Rockerfeller

PLATE 2   Wild *Agaricus campestris*

Bob Harris

PLATE 3
Striate margin of
Psilocybe semilanceata

Alan Rockerfeller

Bob Harris

Alan Rockerfeller

PLATE 4   Sun-dried pellicle of *Psilocybe semilanceata*

Bob Harris

Alan Rockerfeller

PLATE 5 *Panaeolus subbalteatus*

Bob Harris

PLATE 6   Habitat of *Panaeolus subbalteatus*

Bob Harris

Alan Rockerfeller

PLATE 7   Partial veil of *Psilocybe cubensis*

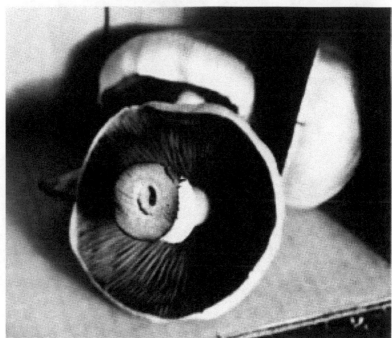

Bob Harris

Alan Rockerfeller

PLATE 8   Bluing reaction of *Psilocybe cubensis*

Bob Harris

PLATE 9 Habitat of *Psilocybe baeocystis*

Bob Harris

Alan Rockerfeller

Plate 10. Habitat of Psilocybe neoxalapensis

**Psilocybe
hoogshagenii**

Alan Rockerfeller

PLATE 10   *Psilocybe baeocystis*

Bob Harris

Alan Rockerfeller

Habitat of Psilocybe caerulescens

PLATE 11   Habitat of *Psilocybe stuntzii*

Bob Harris

Alan Rockerfeller

Habitat of Psilocybe subtropicalis

PLATE 12 Persistent annulus of *Psilocybe stuntzii*

Bob Harris

Alan Rockerfeller

PLATE 13   *Psilocybe cyanescens*

Bob Harris

Alan Rockerfeller

PLATE 14   *Psilocybe cyanescens*

Bob Harris

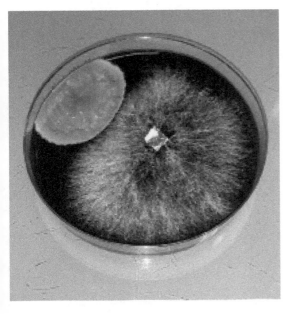

**Hericium erinaceus
and Penicillium**

PLATE 15 *Contaminated Agar plate* Green structure:
Penicillium; white: mycelium of *Ps. cubensis*

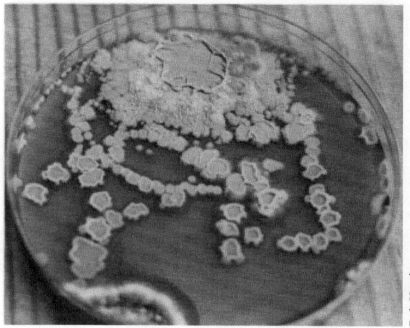

Bob Harris

Ganoderma neojaponicum contamintated with yeast

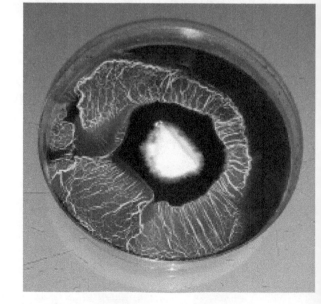

PLATE 16   Yeast-contaminated Agar plate

Starting Cultures

GATHERING MATERIALS

A description has been given so far for all the equipment and food substrates for growing mushrooms. Now you have to obtain a culture start. All that is left then is to inoculate and isolate the pure culture. There are three ways to obtain a start of a culture. The first is simple, get a pure culture from someone — either a friend who has isolated the fungus desired or purchase one from one of the following companies that specializes in the collection and sale of cultures:

> *Northern Regional Research Lab*
> 1815 N. University St.
> Peoria, Ill 61604

> *American Type Culture Collection*
> 12301 Parklawn Drive
> Rockville, MD 20852

> *Centraalbureau voor Schimmelcultures*
> Oosterstraat 1
> Baarn, the Netherlands

The advantage of buying a culture is that you are assured of purity. The disadvantages are cost ($15-$50 a culture) or that the particular strain they are selling is not suitable, which, for a number of reasons, is often the case. For example, the strain might be a healthy, viable culture, but not one which readily forms fruiting bodies.

There are two other methods. The first is by gathering spores and then subsequently germinating them in culture. The advantages are in being able to collect spores in the field and store them until you can get them to culture facilities. This works readily for most mushrooms. I have collected spores and germinated them as much as two years later. The disadvantages are again that it is possible to germinate a spore, cultivate it successfully, and find out that it does not form fruiting bodies (carpophores). With patience, however, you can germinate several cultures and test them for fruiting on grain medium and then select the best culture. Spores can be gathered simply by placing a mature mushroom face down on a clean piece of paper and leaving it over night covered by a bowl. However if one can suspend a mushroom cap over a clean glass plate (one-sixteenth inch or so above the plate) the spores will drop down and no extraneous debris will be on the surface. In any case, spore prints should always be made in gathering field collections.

Commercial mushroom farms often start spawn from spores. In this case a young mushroom is taken with the veil intact. It is swabbed with disinfectant and the annulus removed sterilely. The cap is then suspended in a Petri dish over the agar and the spores allowed to discharge directly onto the agar.

The last method of obtaining material for a culture is perhaps the best and most difficult. It involves picking a fresh fruiting mushroom and bringing it as quickly and cleanly as possible to the culture chamber. All tissues in the life cycle of the mushroom, be it mycelium (spawn) or carpophore (fruiting body), can be grown vegetatively in culture. By taking a fresh mushroom to the culture chamber one has the cleanest part of the life cycle — it is usually a large mass of tissue and not directly enmeshed in substrate, as in the case of the mycelium. The surface is washed with disinfectant (iodine-alcohol solution is ideal). A section is then sterilely removed and transferred to an agar dish.

STERILE TECHNIQUE

The very heart of tissue culture work is *sterile technique*. I have tried to describe everything else first; what is needed, and why. But to describe sterile technique is somewhat difficult. The actual task is not difficult, as you will see in the drawings. What is difficult is overcoming your fears of the unknown; in this case, contamination. Because mistakes are not immediately apparent, nor are the sources of contamination, there is a natural initial over-cautiousness over details which will seem to be important but quite often are extraneous. I think therefore the best way to teach it is to show the movements. Like any meditation, with time you will choose the movements which are most comfortable. The secret is to relax, breathe deeply and focus your consciousness at a certain point in space, e.g., the inoculating loop, while moving with flowing gestures.

SPORE STREAKING ON AGAR

The first and most basic sterile technique is used for streaking solutions of spore onto an agar plate. A clean Petri plate is used for the spores. Either spores or a spore print are soaked in cooled sterile distilled water for several hours. Sterility is not absolute here, so be loose without being sloppy. (See fig. 11)

Now a wire loop is flamed in the burner until red. Remove

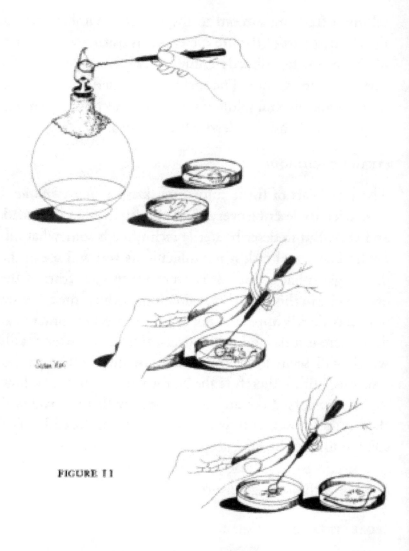

FIGURE 11

the cover of the Petri dish and dip the wire loop into the agar medium. The agar will sizzle and pop and melt until the loop is cool. During this procedure the cover of the Petri plate is held slightly above the plate at an angle as a shield against falling spores. Remove the loop and replace the cover, being careful now not to touch *anything* with the sterile,

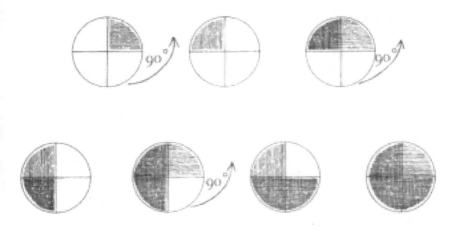

FIGURE 12

cool loop. The loop is then stirred in the spore solution, returned to the Petri plate with the nutrient agar and streaked in a crisscross fashion. The cover is then replaced and the loop flamed again.

Or: Take a flamed loop, cool it, dip it into a spore mass, spore print, or gills of dried carpophore and streak heavily in one quadrant, then rotate the plate 90°. Flame loop, streak a part of quadrant one on quadrant two; continue process in similar fashion for quadrants three and four. (See fig. 12)

An alternate method of spore collection and germination involves a young fruiting body with the veil intact. Special Petri dishes with glass ridges in them are used. The medium is poured so that the agar comes only part way up the height of the ridges. The disinfected young cap with the veil removed is placed upright on the ridges. The spores will then be released onto the agar. The cap can be removed after several hours and the spores allowed to germinate.

STERILE REMOVAL OF TISSUE
FROM FRESHLY GATHERED MUSHROOMS

The alternative and actually, the preferred method, of sterile isolation of mycelium is directly from a mushroom carpophore. The carpophore is disinfected with an alcohol solution of iodine on the surface. The mushroom is placed on a clean surface in the transfer box. A small blade is flamed in the alcohol lamp. Then a section of the carpophore is sliced and removed (a ⅓ inch by ½ inch piece). Flame the knife again and now remove a small piece of tissue from inside the hole just made. This tissue should be sterile, and should be transferred to an agar plate sterilely. The Petri plate agar can be used to cool the blade between flamings as discussed with the loop. The plate can be set aside and the fungus will grow out of this piece of tissue. (See fig. 13)

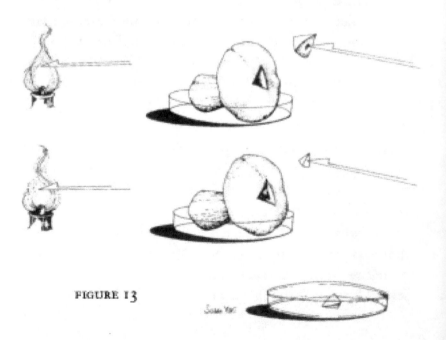

FIGURE 13

TRANSFER FROM THE AGAR MEDIUM

The fungus will grow out on the medium from the spores — or piece of carpophore. This may happen completely with no contaminating fungi; sometimes several fungi will appear along with the desired culture. In any event the culture must be made pure and several platings made for further work. If it is a pure culture a transfer is easy. The knife is flamed and then cooled in the agar in a new sterile plate. Then a section of agar containing the culture is cut out and transferred to the new plate carefully and quickly. If there are other fungi around, care should be taken in removing a small piece of the proper culture as far from the other fungi as possible. Facing it down in the new dish will help prevent the germination of contaminants. (See fig. 14)

Using this technique agar transfers can also be made onto grain medium. You just need to be careful in removing and placing the plugs in the jars or bottles.

While speaking about agar transfers I would like to mention an interesting phenomenon which occurs among fungi. Although cultures can usually be maintained refrigerated for a year, it is necessary to transfer them or they lose vitality; each fungus can change. This is called *sectoring* and can be readily seen on an agar plate as a zone of mycelium that appears different. Some media are better than others for preventing this from happening, the medium of choice depending on the species of fungus. In addition, if a fungus is continually grown on the same medium at constant room temperature, the strain will tend to weaken. That is, if a strain is continually transferred from grain to grain (see next section), after a few transfers there may be a noticeable weakening of the strain. Commercial mushroom farms overcome this by several means. Each culture is taken from an agar plate, transferred to grain, and then used to inoculate

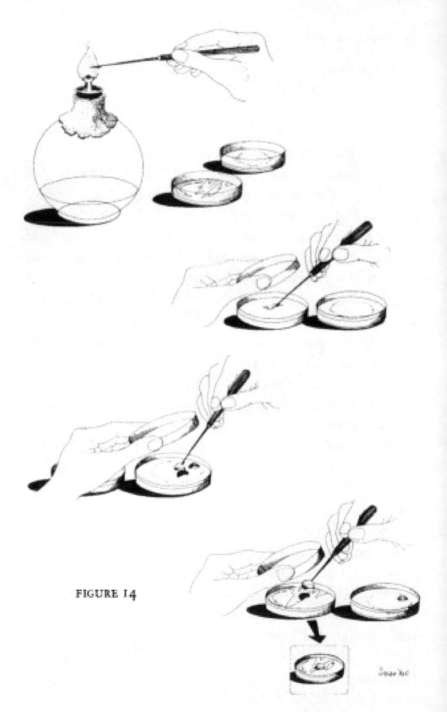

FIGURE 14

all the grain bottles to be used for compost inoculation. So there is only one grain to grain transfer. The problem then becomes how to keep the fungus from weakening on agar. One solution used commercially is to periodically transfer the culture from one agar medium to another. Then, after a time, it can be put back on the original medium. In rather crude form, this is how Armenians kept yogurt bacterial cultures going for years. The culture was routinely passed from one person's house to another where the environment was different. The same procedure apparently works for fungi. The medium must be changed periodically. Another solution is to periodically take a fresh vegetative start from the cap of a mushroom grown on compost. This starts the process anew. Alternately, one can use the spores from a young cap to start a culture or freshen an old one. Here, however, one has added the problem of sexual reproduction and its resulting recombination of genetic material. This could produce a new mutant, different than the parent strain. Why the fungi seem to lose vitality when continually transferred to the same medium is not known. It is postulated that in the wild or on compost the fungus is growing on a heterogeneous material. To interact with the substances in a heterogeneous substrate, the fungus constantly produces a wide array of enzymes to digest the various components of the heterogeneous substrate. This in turn means that the *genome* of the fungus, the entire genetic material, is constantly "tapped" to produce the wide array of enzymes. With constant repetition, a definite pattern is set up. Perhaps with time the fungus loses the ability to readily institute new combinations of the genome when necessary. This may be a simplistic view of the situation, but it merits attention. The essence of a fungus is that it is a non-chlorophyllous plant and as such must have the flexibility to deal with diverse food substrates.

In other plants or animals there is less likelihood for the organism to readily adapt to the changing environment without sexual reproduction. During most of the vegetative stages of the life cycle, higher fungi, such as Basidiomycetes (true mushrooms), have a specialized cell structure in which there are two nuclei for each cell. This is called a *dikaryote*. In most species, there are also connections between the cells, called *clamp connections*. Through these intercellular connections, adjacent cells can swap nuclear material at certain stages of the life cycle. Thus we have asexual genetic recombination. Such genetic recombination without cell replication is called *karyogamy*. In this way higher fungi can undergo mutative changes at a rapid rate.

I hope this diversion from the topic of transferring cultures will give the reader some idea concerning the nature of fungi, so when you are preparing and preserving cultures, and a curious event occurs it may seem a bit more reasonable.

TRANSFER FROM GRAIN TO GRAIN

When agar inoculum has grown out on rye grain, it may be ready for transfer to another bottle sterilely. By shaking cultures on grain periodically (as described in the grain media section), individual grains are encapsulated by the mycelium. These can be shaken and transferred from bottle to bottle. The bottle with inoculum (BI) is clamped on a ringstand in the transfer box with the mouth pointed slightly downward. The plug is removed and the end flamed. A bottle with sterilized media (B) is unplugged and its end flamed. The bottles are placed next to each other, preferably not touching, and the clamped bottle shaken so that a few grains transfer from BI to B. Bottle BI is flamed and the next bottle inoculated. To simplify this transfer I use small mouth soda bottles for BI and transfer to the wider mouth milk

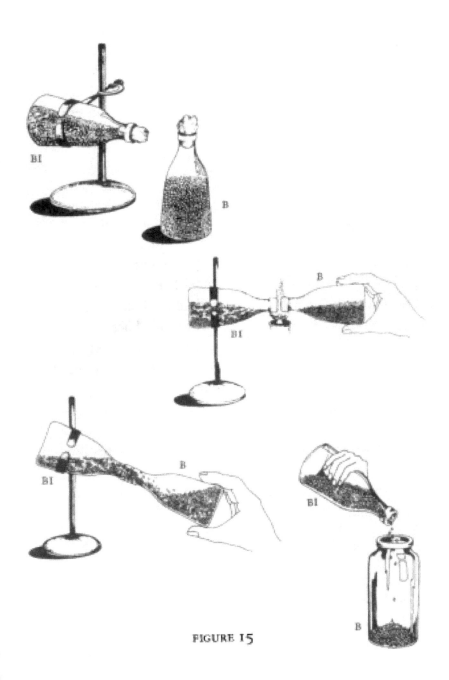

FIGURE 15

bottles. Here one can simply shake the grains from one bottle to the other carefully. (See fig. 15)

Transferring in this fashion (grain to grain) leads to the quickest growth in the new bottle as each rye grain inoculum serves as a point source for new growth. Also cultures seem to lag for a period in moving from agar to grain or any compost medium.

TRANSFER TO COMPOST (NON-STERILE)

The grain-grown cultures can be used to inoculate properly prepared compost for carpophore production. In this case the transfer is done non-sterilely. If the compost is done properly, unlike the grain medium, it will be selective for mushroom growth and resist the growth of a whole multitude of yeast and penicillium type contamination. Therefore, when the compost is laid out (in boxes, bags; whatever area or container) a layer of grain spawn is sprinkled out over the top and covered with a few inches of compost and allowed to incubate for three to four weeks before induction of carpophores (or two if the temperature and humidity are high enough — 55-75°F and a 70-80% humidity, depending on the species).

Alternately, one can mix the grain inoculum (spawn) throughout the entire compost and achieve rapid growth. The faster the mycelium spreads through the compost the less chance of contamination. Thus a heavy inoculation with grain-grown spawn is advantageous. Discovering the best time for compost inoculation seems bewildering at first, but may not be so difficult. Essentially the compost is ready when all the ammonia being formed is driven off. This indicator is used commercially. What this means in reality is that a change has occurred in the nitrogen fixation by the bacteria and fungi (or Actinomycetes) in the compost.

Incubation

AGAR

Once agar plates have been inoculated with spores on a sterile piece of pure culture they may be set aside to grow. I usually stack them in a plastic shoe box or sweater box. I also make a hole in it and plug it with fiberglass. This permits air and humidity but lets no drafts in. It can be left at room temperature or put in an incubator, a lamp will do. A good temperature for all cultures is 72-75°, but some tropical mushrooms will grow at 80°F. Agar cultures prefer a bit less humidity than grain. Also since so much surface is exposed with relation to the size of the opening high moisture environments foster contamination. Leaving the cultures undisturbed as much as possible helps reduce contaminants. By far the chief problems will be with Penicillium-aspergillus type "greenmolds" and yeasts (see plates 15 and 16). The yeasts appear as cream-colored slime on the surface of the agar and spread easily. They also typically have a strong odor. The green molds are masses of the fruiting bodies of the *Penicillium* or *Aspergillus* type fungus. Their sporulation rate is very high and their spores so fine and powdery that they spread easily. Remove and re-isolate or throw out these cultures, or they'll be your bane. To save a mycelial culture on agar from a contaminant, I carefully remove a piece of the mycelium and put it onto a fresh plate. I try to take this piece from an area distant from the contaminant. Sometimes the contaminant can be removed instead, and discarded. I have sometimes encountered *Neurospora*, or bread mold. This is a grey white hairy mass that gets on your plate. It has tiny black fruiting structures that become visible with maturity. The appearance of this fungus is a very tense situation, because it can literally push its way through the lip of the Petri plate and send hyphae out that get spores everywhere. So toss any of these cultures out immediately.

Another frequently encountered contamination is bacteria. These appear as round shiny circles of varied color from pale white to red and orange. When they occur, try to remove them and transfer a piece of the mycelial culture or throw the plate out.

GRAIN

Grain cultures may also be incubated at room temperature or warmer, but the use of a high humidity will increase growth rates. Ninety percent humidity is ideal and can be achieved. An incubator can be easily made by making a bed of kitty litter or gravel in a 2' by 4' container with plastic film as a waterproof liner. A frame is built over it and a poly-ethylene tent is laid over the bed with an opening in the front. Water is put in the gravel bed until saturated and a heating cable with thermostat laid in the bed, resulting in warmth and moisture. The greatest care should be made in seeing that not too much heat is generated, thus a thermostat is useful. (I made one from the control unit of an aquarium heater and spliced it into the heating cable.)

Alternately if one uses narrow mouthed bottles such as soda pop or milk bottles, the incubating grain cultures can be placed on an electric blanket set on medium. Bottom heat will generate enough humidity in these containers.

If the grain is shaken every four to five days, the mycelium, with proper humidity and temperature, will fill the container in two weeks and fruit directly on the spawn. The grain is shaken, preferably, into ½ gallon containers, and then covered with casing mixture. This is not a precise mixture. I like vermiculite, peat moss, crushed oyster shell and fine sand. This is sterilized and cooled before use. A layer ¾ inch thick is spread above the grain and sprayed with cold water so that the layer becomes moist and no water dribbles down into the mycelium. This is tricky but practice will prove important as a teacher. For the next two weeks it must never be allowed to dry out or be too wet. The jars should be in an area a bit cooler perhaps than where the spawn grew out over the grain. If it's too hot, carpophores will form, but

Grain Spawn

Alan Rockefeller

the mycelium will grow up to the surface of the casing layer. Cool moisture forces it to contract to form *rhizomorphs* (strings) and tiny pinheads, the forerunner of fruiting bodies. The areas for grain growth must be ventilated but free of drafts, yet retain humidity. An insulated box with a plastic lid kept slightly ajar may suffice and room temperature may be adequate here, or you may use the incubation chamber described above.

COMPOST

Compost is comparable to grain; when first spawned, it should be warm and humid but without direct moisture. If in boxes, I cover the box with a damp pillow case and then a loose sheet of plastic. Then watering the pillow case lightly provides humidity. If the compost is "alive" (inoculated while still biothermically active) no heat is necessary, at least during the summer. During the colder months of the year

Mushroom compost

it may be necessary to provide heat for the compost, especially while the mycelium is spreading. In some instances I have
grown the mycelium indoors on compost. When doing this,
adequate drainage and air circulation must be maintained.
I have lined the bottoms of fish tanks or plastic containers
with kitty litter or gravel for drainage, spread out the compost, inoculated, and covered it with a plastic sheet. For heat
I used heat lamps overhead. One setup that I have used
successfully in garages has been an old bathtub lined with

Growing mushrooms in compost in tub

kitty litter with a heating cable buried in the litter. Straw and compost covered the litter and a plastic sheet was draped over the tub. After a few weeks the spawn will form a complete layer across the compost. It can then be cased as in the grain method, or even just with dirt. Daily watering is most helpful here — it draws the mycelium to the surface and causes fruiting bodies to form. This casing layer of soil is applied after the mycelium has completely grown out through the compost. It is critical for some, but not all, mushrooms in order for them to form their fruiting bodies. Since this casing layer is not sterilized soil, but rather soil that may have been pasteurized, there is a certain bacteria or algae population present. By keeping the moisture of the casing layer at a constant rate, these bacteria and/or algae multiply. They presumably release certain biochemical compounds that stimulate or trigger the fruiting of some of these mushrooms. It is critical that you keep this layer as evenly moist as possible. This means that spraying a small amount several times a day is preferable to spraying a large amount once a day. It is the consistency of humidity that generates large populations of microbiological organisms, rather than a peak of water and then a lack of it. The actual watering of the casing layer is quite an art and a skilled mushroom farmer can, by controlling the amount and level of water in his casing layer, determine exactly how far up on top of the pile the mushrooms will form their fruiting bodies. It is by controlling the humidity level within that casing layer that you can get the fruiting bodies to be initiated below the surface of the casing layer instead of right on top of the surface. In this way, you can get nice clean picking or picking where the stems are a little bit stronger because they have pushed up through something. Each person must develop his own feel for the art of working with this casing layer. Different mushrooms will require different compositions and pH (acidity) in this casing layer. With some of the wild mushrooms, I have just used plain dirt and it was much more successful than peat moss mixtures, which have high acidity and have to be corrected. Moisture absorption by soil is quicker than with peat moss too.

There are some areas where mushrooms are grown that use an almost pure limestone casing layer. This is very sweet and high in calcium. It might be an advantage to add some crushed oyster shells or some other calcium source which will help to neutralize the pH of this casing layer and, at the same time, add calcium which may be indicated in the fruiting of several of the wild mushrooms. Although some mushrooms start fruiting because of biochemical triggers, many require light in order to initiate mushrooms from mycelium. I am frequently asked by people wanting to grow mushrooms whether they need light or darkness. The cultivated store mushroom *Agaricus brunnescens* does grow in the dark but that is an exception. Most mushrooms do need light. If natural light is not available, artificial light will suffice. Daylight fluorescent lights are preferable to warm white or Gro-Lux, etc. because the pigments in mushrooms responsible for causing fruiting respond better to a bluish type of light. It is on this casing layer that you will see the actual fruiting bodies being formed. Of course there are some mushrooms that do not require casing at all, such as *Pleurotis*. Anywhere from two weeks to a month is required before fruiting starts. It is quite an exciting event to watch a fruiting body go from a tiny little button to a large mass all in a matter of several days. Then flushes will appear for up to three to five months. It has been shown that for some mushrooms — especially those

Agaricus brunnescens

with veils and persistent annuli — that it is advisable to har-
vest mushrooms before the spores are released. For some
fungi these spores inhibit the production of more fruiting
bodies. The mycelium germinating from spores gives off vol-
atile gaseous compounds which stimulate the further growth
of mycelium but inhibits fruiting.

My experience with the fruiting of various mushrooms —
both in cultures and with mushrooms in the wild — seems
to readily follow the phases of the moon. The largest con-
centrations being at or near the new moon until the full
moon.

What I have talked about has been how to take an organism from its natural environment, isolate it, and observe it
for a period of time in an artificial condition. This is a process that has been little talked about in most people's educa-
tion and yet is a rather simple one. The reason for learning
this process of isolating an organism sterilely, a single fun-

gus, is to be able to learn enough about that organism to create the conditions that it grows in naturally, which is to return it to nature. Whenever I do any work, it is with this in mind. How can I duplicate the conditions of nature once I have isolated the organism? In the case of most ground-dwelling mushrooms the question is in making the right compost. What are the right ingredients? What is the right succession of organisms in order to bring about the proper conditions? With this in mind, I do the collecting and then return the fungi to the conditions found in nature. I cannot emphasize enough that it is only when you have truly come to know the organism that you will be able to grow it "in nature". This is the goal of this whole process. While I have not spent a great deal of time discussing composting, it is nonetheless this process that is so critical. I am not an expert on composting and therefore, I cannot begin to say more than I have already said. Yet I feel that this is the basis of all of it, those few words on composting. In a sense, that is the simplest part of the process, once you discover the right in-gredients and the right conditions. This is a matter of trial and error.

One book that comes to mind that is a good source of information on composting is the Rodale book called *The Complete Book of Composting*. There are several short books on growing mushrooms, one of which is by Simmons, *Mushroom Growing*.

With trial and error one can grow most any kind of mush-room, given enough spawn with which to test. Though mushrooms can be grown in bottles and jars, the emphasis should be on compost. Once you work it out for one mush-room, you will need to try others, for all organisms are dif-ferent. The compost or the substrate required for an oyster

Michigan Morels.com

Pleurotis ostreatus

mushroom, *Pleurotis*, the normal log inhabitor, is very different from that of the Shaggy Mane of a *Coprinus*, a normal ground inhabitor. Playing detective and finding out what each mushroom likes is a most rewarding process. It's getting the feeling of another organism that is to be gained. You must be very careful when cultivating mushrooms to identify the mushroom that you are cultivating. For many of you it may mean only getting cultures from the Department of Agriculture. For others who are well versed in mushroom identification it may mean just a walk in the woods. It may mean travelling to a certain place at a certain time to gather certain mushrooms.

Random Field Notes on North American Psilocybin Mushrooms

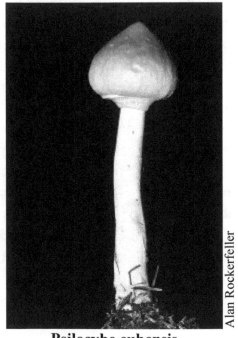

Alan Rockerfeller

Psilocybe cubensis

North American
Psilocybin Mushrooms

I HAVE DECIDED to include a section on North American psilocybin mushrooms for several reasons. Some readers will only be concerned with learning to cultivate mushrooms for food, while others will be decidedly curious about cultivating wild psilocybin mushrooms. My own investigations in this area have left me with the impression that this topic has been rather poorly covered in most texts. The result is that someone might unknowingly cultivate a lethally poisonous mushroom which seemed similar to a description in another book. Part of the problem has been due to poor photographs and a lack of clear identifications of the species by professional mycologists. To put it bluntly, there has not been much interest in identifying all the "little brown mushrooms" (LBM as they have been appropriately called) by the professional community. Therefore, one is bound to get an unclear picture.

Recently, however, mushrooms containing psilocybin have been reported from many diverse habitats and regions of North America. Since there has been a gap in information, I would like to add what I can to this field. This section of the book is *not* intended as a field guide to the species listed, and I would again caution those who do field collections to bring along someone with a thorough knowledge of fungi identification. There are several recently published books which help in the identification of these mushrooms. See the Bibliography at the end of this book for a listing of these and other related books.

To open my discussion of the psilocybin-containing mushrooms, I would like to make some generalizations. Most of the psilocybin-containing mushrooms are in genera which have purple-brown or black spore prints. If you get a mushroom with a rusty brown or white spore print, it may well be something poisonous. Once you have determined that its spore print is purple-brown (for *Psilocybe*) or black (for *Panaeolus*), you then must match descriptions with those available. I would like to add that almost all of the *Psilocybes* (and some of the *Panaeoli*) I have seen exhibit the well-known bluing reaction discussed in almost all the information on these mushrooms. To reiterate, when the base of the stem or, in many cases, the cap is bruised, it turns blue in from five to twenty minutes (see plate 8). A word of caution is necessary here. There are other mushrooms which will turn blue, so this bluing reaction must be found on a mushroom with the right color spore print or it is meaningless. In the literature, there is often a reference to a film developer called metol that enhances this reaction. Again this chemical will react with many mushrooms other than psilocybin-containing mushrooms, so remember to get the spore print first. Once it has been established as a blue-staining *Psilocybe* or *Panaeolus*, one should then try to find out its identity.

I place most of my faith in some biochemical assay methods that are currently being worked out for identification of these species, and in classical fungal morphology. Using these two methods in pinpointing, it is possible to decide fairly accurately exactly what species it is that one is dealing with. I have spent more time in developing procedures than in getting a varied selection or knowledge of the different species. Hopefully, with time and support (finances), I will be able to use these methods to establish identity in other species. I have become aware in my travels that there are species of psilocybin mushrooms around which are unknown by people in that area or, if known, have not been reported in the journals. In some cases, there may be one isolated collection which is never heard from again. My own personal encounters and experiences in gathering them for collections has been rather limited. I must say however, that mine has been a rather unique situation.

PSILOCYBE CUBENSIS, *Plates 7 and* 8.

The first instance of my gathering psilocybin-containing mushrooms was of the large strain called *Psilocybe cubensis*. This is the more common *Psilocybe* found in the tropical, semi-tropical environments throughout Georgia, Florida, Louisiana, Texas and some parts of Tennessee, on down through Mexico and South America as far as Peru. It has been reported in Thailand and Cambodia, and in Cuba as well. I have seen fruiting bodies that weigh up to a quarter of a pound, being ten inches across in some varieties like the specimens pictured here and in the color plates, the darker strain from Palenque, Mexico. The first one I ever saw was in a field with Brahmin cows in Colombia, outside the city of Cali. It was my fortune to be travelling with my dear friend, Dr. Andrew Weil. The characteristics for identifying it were readily verifiable. The stem and the cap readily turn blue when bruised. It has a rather large fruiting body, anywhere from two to ten inches across. The stem is ½ inch to

Alan Rockerfeller

Psilocybe cubensis

an inch in diameter. It has a veil that tears upon the opening
of the cap in the same way that a regular mushroom does.
The veil remains on the stem as an annulus and frequently
appears black. This is a rather important characteristic. The
spore print is purple, almost purple-black. It is found on cow
pies and is pretty much limited to the southeast in the United
States. The mushroom is not actually growing on the cow
dung. What is happening is that the cow pie has landed on
the grass and in a matter of time the nitrogen, and the water,
and the bacterial action rot the grass under the cow pie, the
major compost heap. This can occur in warm climates because there is no need for all the insulation that a compost

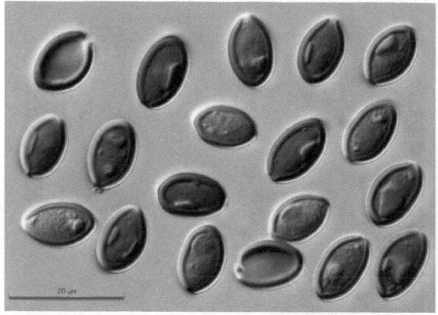

Spores of Psilocybe cubensis

Alan Rockerfeller

heap has. The cow pie acts as a temperature and humidity regulating device. The spores germinate on the grass and the result is that it spreads throughout the composted grass and pokes its way through the cow pie.

PSILOCYBE SEMILANCEATA, *Plates 3 and 4.*

It wasn't until several years later that I saw any other species. Again, it was with Dr. Weil. He was in Oregon at the time and had been collecting the rather widely-known coastal Oregon species called the Liberty Cap, or *Psilocybe semilanceata*, which I had never collected, and I wanted to learn its characteristics firsthand. *Psilocybe semilanceata* is found along the coast from the southern Oregon border north through British Columbia. As I said, I had the fortune of collecting with Dr. Weil, who is on the Harvard Botanical Museum Contributing Staff. It took quite a while to learn the characteristics of this organism and I have included several photographs in this book to depict the broad variation of this species. Many of the North American species that I will be talking about share this characteristic of broad variation. *Ps. semilanceata* frequently has a bell-shaped pointed cap, and it is long and slender. It has a very thin, long stem (about three inches long) and may be a sixteenth of an inch in diameter. The cap has lines running down it that are visible when the cap is moist, called *striations*. It has a striate

Alan Rockerfeller

**Psilocybe
Semilanceata**

Alan Rockerfeller

margin. One of the more outstanding characteristics is apparent when the moist cap is broken into pieces and a piece is taken between the fingertips. Bend it back, and strip off a thin film that covers the cap, the *viscid pellicle*. If it has been in the sun, it will dry up and the cap will appear white. In that case it does not have the pellicle or that filmy consistency that can be peeled back. The particular environment that *Ps. semilanceata* grows best in appears to be on the compost

formed by the dead sedge grass from previous years at the
base of growing sedge clumps. Sedge grass grows in clumps
anywhere from the central Willamette Valley to the coast,
and is recognizable by the long, triangular needle-shaped
leaves. During the rainy season, which is anywhere from
September on, the mushrooms appear in old fields that have
been grazed on a few years ago, but have not seen too much
grazing this year. In these clumps, or at the base where there

Psilocybe semilanceata in sedge clump

is grey, rotted straw from previous years, they grow out with
long stems. The fruiting of most of these mushrooms is trig-
gered by light. *Ps. semilanceata* has a greyish-lilac spore
print. Occasionally, you will pick one and see a bluing at
the base, but usually they don't blue when bruised. One of
the characteristics that people sometimes use is that the stem
is rather elastic. I do not use this as a determining character-

istic, but I do use the viscid pellicle. When hunting *Ps. semilanceata*, which is quite small and unnoticeable or, more often than not, hidden in the clump of sedge grass, I use what I refer to as the sentry technique. I walk along the fields at a moderate pace looking for an obvious one or two mushrooms growing more or less out in the open. Then I bend down and part the grass or move the compost around until I find more. This mushroom has a tendency to grow in clusters, though it can also be solitary.

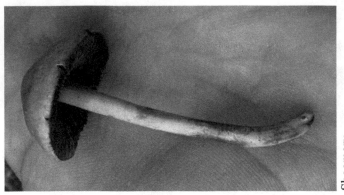

Panaeolus subbalteatus (white fuzz on stem)

PANAEOLUS SUBBALTEATUS, *Plates 5 and 6.*

Panaeolus subbalteatus usually fruits in the springtime in the Willamette Valley in Oregon and from upstate New York to Florida in manured cornfields and hay piles. It has a widely-varied coloration, shape and formation. It will grow singly and in clusters. It will be dark brown with a sort of rusty brown on the cap and a thin stripe of darker, more chocolate brown around the edge, and will range from an almost dome shape, typical *Panaeolus* umbo, to a flat cap that is around two inches across. It has a slightly depressed edge outside the umbo and a flattened edge which is dark brown with a lighter center which turns black when dry.

The spore print is black. This *Panaeolus* can have wrinkles and be shiny when dry, with a sort of white fuzz on the stem that has ridges spiralling up to the cap. Usually, there is bluing of the mycelium at the base of the stem when it is bruised.

Psilocybe pelliculosa

PSILOCYBE PELLICULOSA

Psilocybe pelliculosa (as recently described in Alexan. Smith's new *A Field Guide to Western Mushrooms*) i rather small, inconspicuous brown mushroom quite sim in shape and appearance to *Psilocybe semilanceata*. It li wise is small, has a striate margin and a separable pellicle seems to turn blue more easily than *Ps. semilanceata* on bruising. The cap color seems a bit paler and the flesh a bit more delicate. It grows at the edge of forests, i.e., where the grass of the meadow meets a forest; sometimes it appears in the moss on rotting logs. It would be a rather difficult mushroom to identify at first, but since it stains blue, one can be sure that if the one you have doesn't blue, it's not the right one. As far as I know, the habitat is confined to the Pacific Northwest.

Psilocybe baeocystis

PSILOCYBE BAEOCYSTIS, *Plates* 9 *and* 10.

I have found *Psilocybe baeocystis* growing on conifer mulch in the state of Washington. It was smaller than the other two bark-inhabiting species I found (see below). It has a hemispherical-shaped cap, and shows no convolutions with age. It exhibited a viscid pellicle which appears white after drying, but striations were not evident at the margin. It blued

very easily upon contact. The spore print is a greyish-purple
to lilac. This species is rather rare, but interesting because
of the various alkaloids present. Though not often encountered, when found, the fruiting is often profuse. This variety
is also quite potent for its size.

Psilocybe stuntzii

PSILOCYBE STUNTZII, *Plates* 11 *and* 12.

This mushroom has been growing on the University of
Washington campus. It came in on the bark mulch and,
for several years, was there and available. Eventually the
school changed their mulch supplier so that they wouldn't
have to deal with the problem of psychedelic mushrooms on
their campus. This is a fairly good-sized mushroom. It gets
up to two inches across at most and may be as small as half
an inch. It has a stiff, thick persistent annulus on the stem.

Alan Rockerfeller

Psilocybe allenii
P. stunzii and P. allenii are closely related and
both grow in wood chips

The cap has a viscid pellicle and a striate margin, but when
fully opened, it is in a flat position with a rather curved edge;
in other words, the edges are almost scalloped all the way
around. It has a greyish-purple spore print. This is a rather
fibrous mushroom and has a meatier texture than any of the
other *Psilocybes* I collected. This species seems to be among
the less potent for its weight. I have seen it growing on lawns
on which bark mulch has been used. I have seen and collected this variety in Oregon and Washington only.

PSILOCYBE CYANESCENS, *Plates* 13 *and* 14.

This species grows in the conifer mulch similar to *Psilocybe
stuntzii*. It has a fleshy stem and a striate margin. The margin is typically convoluted with age. This mushroom turns

Caleb Brown

Psilocybe cyanescens

blue almost immediately upon contact. However, there is
no annulus which remains on the stem. It has a greyish-
purple spore print. It appears to be chemically different from
Psilocybe stuntzii, and is, in fact, one of the most potent
Psilocybe mushrooms. Single collections of up to 100 pounds
have been found on lawns in Washington.

fungiflora.com

Psilocybe cyanescens

I HAVE GIVEN what information I could about the few species I've seen, and provided what I consider to be fairly good photographs. I have tried, out of the knowledge that I have, to state the key information that would be useful in identifying those mushrooms to be collected and those to be avoided. When collecting, prime importance must be placed on proper identification, for the poisonous varieties are often quite similar to those you may be seeking. I know of no complete work in this area to date. I have learned more from information and photographs sent to me by others than from the published literature.

bonga 1965

Facts About Mushrooms

By Mushroompeople

Mushrooms are ecologically important

Many plants owe their existence to fungi. Green plants perform the miracle of transforming sunlight, water, and carbon dioxide into living material by photosynthesis, but they cannot break down insolubles (e.g. rock) into soluble forms. On the other hand, fungi cannot make carbohydrates (sugars and starches), but can break down minerals into soluble nitrates, phosphates, and sulphates vital to plants. Plants and fungi evolved over the aeons in a symbiosis called mycorrhizal. Without some fungi, many plants die. Without the plants, fungi do not thrive.

Mushrooms are a sustainable forest product

If you love forests, make them cost-effective. In Tennessee we show our neighbors how log-grown shiitake are profitable. Sustainable tree harvesting benefits the woods by releasing healthy trees from competition by weaker ones, thus growing a climax forest faster than nature can do it alone.

Mushrooms are nutritious

Shiitake is 13-18% protein dry weight, high in leucine and lysine (scarce in most grains), and a good complement of minerals and vitamins. Many mushrooms are equally nutritious. The familiar Oyster can be grown in straw, sawdust, coffee grounds, and other agri-waste products, and show a potential for helping feed the world.

Mushrooms are the ultimate health food

In Japan shiitake is routinely used as part of cancer treatment. Reishi and Maitake (hen of the woods) produce strong benefits to the immune system and lower cholesterol. Fungi make the familiar antibiotics to compete with other microorganisms

Mushroom Books

Alexopoulos, Constantine J., *Introductory Mycology*, Wiley & Sons. A well-documented, logical and clear explanation of the structure and classification of fungi along with an introduction to physiological, biochemical, genetic and ecological data on mushrooms and other fungi.

Chilton, J.S. and Paul Stamets, *Mushroom Cultivator: A Practical Guide to Growing Mushrooms at Home*, Agarikon Press. The classic "Bible" for all phases of mushroom cultivation and expert compost-making. The growing parameters are given for many species, with excellent sections on pests and troubleshooting.

Gartz, Jochen, *Magic Mushrooms Around the World*, Luna Information Services. Introducing a rich variety of psychoactive mushrooms from around the globe— including some rare and little-known species. The author describes dozens of species and covers a broad range of mushroom-related topics, from distribution maps to comparisons of cultural attitudes to laboratory analyses of active ingredients.

Laessoe, Thomas. and Gary Lincoff, G. *Mushrooms: A Smithsonian Handbook*, Dorling Kindersley Publishing. One of the most beautiful books around, with 2,300 color photos of over 500 species and 304 pages.

Lincoff, Gary. *The Audubon Field Guide to North American Mushrooms*, Knopf. With more than 700 mushrooms detailed with color photographs and descriptive text, this is the most comprehensive photographic field guide to the mushrooms of North America.

McKenna, Terence, *The Archaic Revival: Speculations on Psychedelic Mushrooms, the Amazon, Virtual Reality, UFOs, Evolution.* Harper SanFrancisco. In this spiritual journey, McKenna ponders shamanism, buddhism, and enthnopharmacology. By the phrase "archaic revival," he refers to a return to shamanism, which he believes can be enhanced by current scientific practices.

Miller, Orson, *Mushrooms of North America,* Dutton. This is a flexible field guide and is comprehensive and has full-color pictures of mushrooms. It has a how, when and where to collect mushrooms. The book has a key to determine the exact species, a bibliography and a special section on mushroom toxins.

Reidlinger, T., (ed.), *The Sacred Mushroom Seeker: Tributes to R. Wasson,* Inner Traditions. The adventures of banker-scientist J. Gordon Wasson, who discovered the shamanic use of entheogenic mushrooms in Oaxaca, Mexico. Articles by Terence McKenna, Peter Furst, Albert Hoffman, Richard Shultes, & others.

Stamets, Paul, *Growing Gourmet and Medicinal Mushrooms*, 3rd Edition, Ten Speed Press. The state-of-the-art manual for cultivating edible and medicinal mushrooms, including new ones introduced into cultivation by the author. It includes detailed growing parameters for 7 species of oysters, shiitake, maitake, reishi, the agarici, and many others. Beautiful color photos and illustrations.

Stamets, Paul, *Psilocybin Mushrooms of the World*, Ten Speed Press. The ancients used these amazing fungi as sacraments and intelligence-boosters. An identification guide that covers the whole world. Beautiful color electron microphotography.

Books for Independent Minds

Visit roninpub.com, review our great books,
get book isbn and order from any bookstore.

CPSIA information can be obtained
at www.ICGtesting.com
Printed in the USA
JSHW031837110123
36141JS00018B/1222